50 Taste of Japan Dishes

By: Kelly Johnson

Table of Contents

- Sushi
- Ramen
- Tempura
- Tonkatsu
- Okonomiyaki
- Udon
- Sashimi
- Miso Soup
- Teriyaki Chicken
- Takoyaki
- Donburi
- Bento Box
- Shabu-Shabu
- Katsu Curry
- Gyoza
- Sukiyaki
- Chawanmushi
- Ebi Nigiri
- Tamagoyaki
- Kiritanpo
- Oyakodon
- Yaki Udon
- Maki Rolls
- Onigiri
- Nikujaga
- Tofu Katsu
- Unagi Don
- Chirashi Sushi
- Zaru Soba
- Nabe
- Edamame
- Ebi Tempura
- Kaiseki
- Tori Karaage
- Ebi Chili

- Kushiage
- Goma-ae
- Hiyayakko
- Kinpira Gobo
- Japanese Curry
- Takikomi Gohan
- Oden
- Chashu Pork
- Kakiage
- Mochi
- Daifuku
- Anmitsu
- Taiyaki
- Matcha Cake
- Yuzu Sorbet

Sushi

Ingredients:

- 2 cups sushi rice
- 2 cups water
- 2 tablespoons rice vinegar
- 1 tablespoon sugar
- 1/2 teaspoon salt
- 10-12 sheets nori (seaweed)
- Fresh fish (salmon, tuna, etc.), thinly sliced
- Cucumber, julienned
- Avocado, sliced
- Soy sauce, for dipping

Instructions:

1. **Prepare the Rice:** Rinse the sushi rice under cold water until the water runs clear. Combine rice and water in a pot, then bring to a boil. Reduce heat, cover, and simmer for 20 minutes. Let the rice sit, covered, for 10 more minutes.
2. **Season the Rice:** Mix rice vinegar, sugar, and salt until dissolved. Gently fold the vinegar mixture into the cooked rice. Allow it to cool to room temperature.
3. **Assemble the Sushi:** Place a sheet of nori on a bamboo sushi mat. Spread a thin layer of rice over the nori, leaving a 1-inch border at the top. Add your choice of fillings (fish, cucumber, avocado). Roll the sushi tightly using the mat.
4. **Serve:** Slice the roll into bite-sized pieces and serve with soy sauce and wasabi.

Ramen

Ingredients:

- 4 cups chicken broth
- 2 cups water
- 2 tablespoons soy sauce
- 1 tablespoon miso paste
- 1 tablespoon sesame oil
- 2 servings ramen noodles
- 2 boiled eggs
- 1/2 cup sliced green onions
- 1/4 cup bamboo shoots (optional)
- 1/2 cup cooked chicken or pork slices
- 1/4 cup nori strips

Instructions:

1. **Prepare the Broth:** In a pot, combine chicken broth, water, soy sauce, miso paste, and sesame oil. Bring to a simmer and cook for 10 minutes.
2. **Cook the Noodles:** Cook ramen noodles according to package instructions. Drain and set aside.
3. **Assemble the Ramen:** Divide cooked noodles between bowls. Pour the hot broth over the noodles. Top with boiled egg, green onions, bamboo shoots, protein (chicken or pork), and nori.
4. **Serve:** Garnish with additional toppings like sesame seeds, chili oil, or sprouts.

Tempura

Ingredients:

- 1 cup all-purpose flour
- 1/2 cup cornstarch
- 1 teaspoon baking powder
- 1/4 teaspoon salt
- 1 cup ice-cold water
- 10 shrimp, peeled and deveined
- 1 zucchini, sliced
- 1 sweet potato, sliced
- Vegetable oil, for frying
- Soy sauce, for dipping

Instructions:

1. **Make the Batter:** In a bowl, mix flour, cornstarch, baking powder, and salt. Add ice-cold water and stir until just combined.
2. **Heat the Oil:** Heat oil in a deep pot or wok to 350°F.
3. **Fry the Tempura:** Dip shrimp and vegetables in the batter and fry in the hot oil until golden and crispy, about 2-3 minutes for shrimp and 4-5 minutes for vegetables.
4. **Serve:** Drain on paper towels and serve with soy sauce for dipping.

Tonkatsu

Ingredients:

- 4 pork cutlets (boneless)
- 1/2 cup flour
- 2 eggs, beaten
- 1 cup panko breadcrumbs
- Vegetable oil, for frying
- Tonkatsu sauce (store-bought or homemade)

Instructions:

1. **Prepare the Pork:** Season the pork cutlets with salt and pepper. Dredge each cutlet in flour, dip in beaten eggs, and coat in panko breadcrumbs.
2. **Fry the Tonkatsu:** Heat oil in a frying pan over medium heat. Fry the cutlets for 4-5 minutes per side until golden brown and cooked through.
3. **Serve:** Drain on paper towels and serve with tonkatsu sauce.

Okonomiyaki

Ingredients:

- 1 cup flour
- 1/2 cup dashi broth (or water)
- 1 egg
- 1 cup shredded cabbage
- 1/2 cup cooked pork or shrimp, diced
- 2 tablespoons green onions, chopped
- 1 tablespoon vegetable oil
- Okonomiyaki sauce (or tonkatsu sauce)
- Kewpie mayonnaise

Instructions:

1. **Make the Batter:** In a bowl, combine flour, dashi broth, egg, cabbage, pork (or shrimp), and green onions. Mix well.
2. **Cook the Okonomiyaki:** Heat a skillet over medium heat and lightly oil it. Pour the batter onto the skillet, forming a round pancake. Cook for 4-5 minutes per side until golden brown and cooked through.
3. **Serve:** Drizzle with okonomiyaki sauce and mayo. Garnish with bonito flakes or seaweed (optional).

Udon

Ingredients:

- 4 cups dashi broth
- 2 tablespoons soy sauce
- 1 tablespoon mirin
- 2 servings udon noodles
- 2 boiled eggs
- 1/4 cup sliced green onions
- 1/4 cup sliced mushrooms (optional)

Instructions:

1. **Prepare the Broth:** In a pot, combine dashi broth, soy sauce, and mirin. Bring to a simmer for 10 minutes.
2. **Cook the Noodles:** Cook the udon noodles according to package instructions. Drain and set aside.
3. **Assemble the Udon:** Place noodles in bowls, pour the hot broth over, and garnish with sliced green onions, mushrooms, and boiled eggs.
4. **Serve:** Enjoy hot with additional seasonings as desired.

Sashimi

Ingredients:

- Fresh sashimi-grade fish (salmon, tuna, etc.)
- Soy sauce
- Wasabi
- Pickled ginger

Instructions:

1. **Prepare the Fish:** Using a sharp knife, slice the fish into thin pieces.
2. **Serve:** Arrange the sashimi on a plate, and serve with soy sauce, wasabi, and pickled ginger.

Miso Soup

Ingredients:

- 4 cups dashi broth
- 2 tablespoons miso paste
- 1/4 cup tofu, cubed
- 2 tablespoons sliced green onions
- 1 tablespoon wakame seaweed (optional)

Instructions:

1. **Prepare the Soup:** In a pot, heat dashi broth over medium heat. Once hot, add miso paste and stir until dissolved.
2. **Add the Tofu:** Gently add tofu and wakame (if using) to the soup and simmer for 5 minutes.
3. **Serve:** Garnish with sliced green onions and serve.

Teriyaki Chicken

Ingredients:

- 2 chicken breasts
- 1/4 cup soy sauce
- 2 tablespoons brown sugar
- 1 tablespoon rice vinegar
- 1 tablespoon sesame oil
- 1 garlic clove, minced
- 1 teaspoon ginger, grated
- 1 tablespoon cornstarch (optional for thickening)

Instructions:

1. **Make the Teriyaki Sauce:** In a saucepan, combine soy sauce, brown sugar, rice vinegar, sesame oil, garlic, and ginger. Simmer for 5-7 minutes, allowing the sauce to thicken. If desired, mix cornstarch with a little water and add to the sauce to thicken further.
2. **Cook the Chicken:** Grill or pan-fry the chicken breasts until fully cooked.
3. **Serve:** Brush the cooked chicken with teriyaki sauce and serve with rice or vegetables.

Takoyaki

Ingredients:

- 1 cup all-purpose flour
- 1 1/2 cups dashi broth
- 2 eggs
- 1/4 cup pickled ginger, chopped
- 1/4 cup tempura scraps (tenkasu)
- 1/2 cup cooked octopus, chopped
- 2 tablespoons green onions, chopped
- Takoyaki sauce (or okonomiyaki sauce)
- Kewpie mayonnaise
- Bonito flakes (optional)
- Aonori (dried seaweed, optional)
- Oil for greasing the pan

Instructions:

1. **Prepare the Batter:** In a bowl, whisk together flour, dashi broth, and eggs until smooth.
2. **Preheat the Takoyaki Pan:** Heat a takoyaki pan over medium heat and lightly grease each hole with oil.
3. **Fill the Pan:** Pour the batter into the holes, filling each about halfway. Add a small amount of octopus, pickled ginger, tempura scraps, and green onions. Fill the rest of the way with batter.
4. **Cook the Takoyaki:** Using chopsticks or a skewer, turn the balls as they cook to form a round shape. Cook for 4-5 minutes, turning regularly, until golden and crispy on the outside.
5. **Serve:** Drizzle with takoyaki sauce and mayonnaise. Sprinkle bonito flakes and aonori on top before serving.

Donburi

Ingredients:

- 1 cup cooked rice
- 1/2 lb chicken, beef, or pork (sliced thin)
- 1/4 cup soy sauce
- 1/4 cup mirin
- 1/4 cup dashi broth or water
- 1 tablespoon sugar
- 1/2 onion, thinly sliced
- 2 eggs
- 2 tablespoons green onions, chopped

Instructions:

1. **Cook the Meat:** In a pan, heat oil and cook the sliced meat until browned.
2. **Prepare the Sauce:** Add soy sauce, mirin, dashi broth, and sugar to the pan, stirring until the sauce begins to simmer. Add the onions and cook until soft.
3. **Add the Eggs:** Beat the eggs and pour them over the meat mixture. Cover the pan and cook until the eggs are set but still soft.
4. **Assemble the Donburi:** Spoon the rice into a bowl and top with the cooked meat and egg mixture. Garnish with green onions.
5. **Serve:** Enjoy warm!

Bento Box

Ingredients:

- 1 cup cooked rice
- 1/2 cup teriyaki chicken or beef
- 1/2 cup tamagoyaki (Japanese omelet)
- 1/2 cup pickled vegetables (like pickled radish or cucumbers)
- 1/2 cup steamed or sautéed vegetables (broccoli, carrots, etc.)
- 1/2 cup fruit (grapes, apple slices, etc.)

Instructions:

1. **Prepare the Ingredients:** Cook rice, prepare teriyaki chicken or beef, make tamagoyaki, and steam or sauté vegetables.
2. **Assemble the Bento Box:** Place rice in one section of the box, add the teriyaki chicken or beef, tamagoyaki, pickled vegetables, and fruit.
3. **Serve:** Close the bento box and enjoy!

Shabu-Shabu

Ingredients:

- 1 lb thinly sliced beef (or pork)
- 4 cups dashi broth
- 1/2 cup soy sauce
- 1 tablespoon sesame oil
- 1 tablespoon mirin
- 1/4 cup green onions, chopped
- Assorted vegetables (bok choy, mushrooms, tofu, carrots, etc.)
- Dipping sauces: Ponzu, sesame dipping sauce

Instructions:

1. **Prepare the Broth:** In a pot, combine dashi broth, soy sauce, sesame oil, and mirin. Bring to a simmer.
2. **Prepare the Ingredients:** Arrange the beef, vegetables, and tofu on plates.
3. **Cook the Ingredients:** Bring the broth to a boil. Quickly dip the slices of beef and vegetables into the hot broth until cooked (about 10-30 seconds for beef, longer for vegetables).
4. **Serve:** Serve with dipping sauces on the side.

Katsu Curry

Ingredients:

- 2 chicken or pork cutlets (breaded and fried)
- 1/2 onion, chopped
- 2 carrots, chopped
- 2 potatoes, cubed
- 2 tablespoons curry powder
- 2 tablespoons soy sauce
- 2 tablespoons ketchup
- 2 cups chicken broth
- 1 tablespoon oil
- 1 cup cooked rice

Instructions:

1. **Cook the Vegetables:** In a pan, heat oil and sauté the onion until softened. Add carrots and potatoes and cook for a few minutes.
2. **Prepare the Curry Sauce:** Add curry powder, soy sauce, ketchup, and chicken broth to the pan. Bring to a boil, then simmer until the vegetables are tender and the sauce thickens.
3. **Cook the Katsu:** Fry the breaded pork or chicken cutlets until golden and cooked through.
4. **Assemble the Dish:** Serve the katsu over rice, then pour the curry sauce over the top.

Gyoza

Ingredients:

- 1/2 lb ground pork
- 1/2 cup cabbage, finely chopped
- 1 tablespoon soy sauce
- 1 tablespoon sesame oil
- 1 garlic clove, minced
- 1 teaspoon grated ginger
- 30 gyoza wrappers
- Vegetable oil for frying
- Soy sauce and vinegar for dipping

Instructions:

1. **Make the Filling:** In a bowl, mix ground pork, cabbage, soy sauce, sesame oil, garlic, and ginger.
2. **Assemble the Gyoza:** Place a small amount of filling in the center of each wrapper, then fold and pleat the edges to seal.
3. **Cook the Gyoza:** Heat oil in a pan over medium heat. Fry the gyoza until the bottom is golden brown. Add a splash of water and cover to steam for 3-4 minutes.
4. **Serve:** Serve with dipping sauce.

Sukiyaki

Ingredients:

- 1 lb thinly sliced beef
- 1/2 onion, sliced
- 1/2 block tofu, cubed
- 1/2 cup shiitake mushrooms, sliced
- 1/4 cup soy sauce
- 1/4 cup mirin
- 2 tablespoons sugar
- 1/4 cup sake
- 2 cups dashi broth
- 2 eggs (for dipping)

Instructions:

1. **Prepare the Broth:** In a pot, combine soy sauce, mirin, sugar, sake, and dashi broth. Bring to a simmer.
2. **Cook the Ingredients:** Add beef, onions, tofu, mushrooms, and other vegetables to the pot. Simmer until the beef is cooked and vegetables are tender.
3. **Serve:** Serve with a raw egg for dipping and enjoy!

Chawanmushi

Ingredients:

- 2 eggs
- 1 cup dashi broth
- 1 tablespoon soy sauce
- 1 teaspoon mirin
- 1/4 cup cooked chicken, shrimp, or mushrooms
- 1/4 teaspoon salt

Instructions:

1. **Make the Egg Mixture:** In a bowl, whisk together eggs, dashi broth, soy sauce, mirin, and salt.
2. **Prepare the Ingredients:** Place chicken, shrimp, or mushrooms in small heatproof cups.
3. **Steam the Chawanmushi:** Pour the egg mixture into the cups, then cover them with foil. Steam over low heat for 15-20 minutes or until the custard is set.
4. **Serve:** Garnish with additional toppings, if desired.

Ebi Nigiri

Ingredients:

- 8-10 cooked shrimp
- 2 cups sushi rice
- 1/4 cup rice vinegar
- 1 tablespoon sugar
- 1/2 teaspoon salt
- 2-3 sheets nori (optional)

Instructions:

1. **Prepare the Rice:** Cook sushi rice and mix it with rice vinegar, sugar, and salt. Let it cool.
2. **Form the Nigiri:** Wet your hands with water and shape a small amount of rice into an oval shape.
3. **Assemble the Nigiri:** Place a shrimp on top of each rice ball. Optionally, wrap a small strip of nori around the rice and shrimp.
4. **Serve:** Serve with soy sauce and wasabi.

Tamagoyaki (Japanese Rolled Omelette)

Ingredients:

- 4 eggs
- 1 tablespoon soy sauce
- 1 tablespoon mirin
- 1 teaspoon sugar
- 1 tablespoon dashi (optional)
- 1 tablespoon vegetable oil (for greasing)

Instructions:

1. **Prepare the Egg Mixture:** In a bowl, whisk the eggs with soy sauce, mirin, sugar, and dashi until smooth.
2. **Cook the Omelette:** Heat a tamagoyaki pan or a regular non-stick pan over medium-low heat. Lightly grease the pan with oil.
3. **Make Layers:** Pour a small amount of egg mixture into the pan, tilting the pan to spread it evenly. Once the egg starts to set but is still slightly runny on top, roll it up into a cylinder.
4. **Add More Layers:** Push the rolled omelette to one side of the pan and add more egg mixture, lifting the rolled part to let the new mixture flow underneath. Once set, roll it up again. Continue this process until all the egg mixture is used.
5. **Shape and Slice:** Let the tamagoyaki cool slightly before slicing it into thick pieces. Serve as a side dish or in bento boxes.

Kiritanpo (Grilled Rice Skewers)

Ingredients:

- 2 cups cooked short-grain rice
- 1/4 cup dashi broth
- 1 tablespoon soy sauce
- 1 tablespoon mirin
- 2-3 skewers

Instructions:

1. **Shape the Rice:** While the rice is still warm, divide it into small portions. Mold the rice around skewers to form cylindrical shapes.
2. **Grill the Skewers:** Lightly grill the rice skewers over medium heat until golden brown and crispy on the outside.
3. **Prepare the Glaze:** In a bowl, combine dashi, soy sauce, and mirin to make a glaze.
4. **Brush the Skewers:** Brush the grilled rice skewers with the glaze and grill for another minute or two, allowing the glaze to caramelize.
5. **Serve:** Serve warm with a sprinkle of sesame seeds or chopped green onions.

Oyakodon (Chicken and Egg Rice Bowl)

Ingredients:

- 2 boneless, skinless chicken thighs, cut into bite-sized pieces
- 1/2 onion, thinly sliced
- 2 eggs, lightly beaten
- 1/4 cup soy sauce
- 1/4 cup mirin
- 1/4 cup dashi broth
- 1 tablespoon sugar
- 2 cups cooked rice
- Green onions, chopped (optional)

Instructions:

1. **Cook the Chicken:** In a skillet, cook the chicken and onions with soy sauce, mirin, dashi, and sugar over medium heat until the chicken is cooked through.
2. **Add the Eggs:** Pour the beaten eggs over the chicken mixture, cover, and cook on low heat until the eggs are just set, but still soft.
3. **Serve:** Spoon the chicken and egg mixture over bowls of rice. Garnish with chopped green onions if desired.

Yaki Udon (Stir-fried Udon Noodles)

Ingredients:

- 2 cups cooked udon noodles
- 1 tablespoon sesame oil
- 1/2 onion, sliced
- 1/2 bell pepper, julienned
- 1/2 carrot, julienned
- 2 cloves garlic, minced
- 1 tablespoon soy sauce
- 1 tablespoon oyster sauce
- 1 tablespoon mirin
- 2 green onions, chopped
- Sesame seeds (optional)

Instructions:

1. **Prepare the Vegetables:** In a large skillet or wok, heat sesame oil over medium heat. Add the onion, bell pepper, carrot, and garlic, and sauté until softened.
2. **Add the Noodles:** Add the cooked udon noodles to the pan and stir-fry for a few minutes to heat through.
3. **Add the Sauce:** In a small bowl, mix the soy sauce, oyster sauce, and mirin. Pour the sauce over the noodles and stir to coat.
4. **Serve:** Garnish with green onions and sesame seeds. Serve hot.

Maki Rolls (Sushi Rolls)

Ingredients:

- 2 cups sushi rice, cooked
- 1/4 cup rice vinegar
- 1 tablespoon sugar
- 1 teaspoon salt
- Nori sheets
- Fillings of your choice (e.g., cucumber, avocado, crab, tuna, salmon, etc.)
- Soy sauce for dipping

Instructions:

1. **Prepare the Rice:** Mix the rice vinegar, sugar, and salt in a small bowl and stir until dissolved. Once the rice has cooled, gently fold this mixture into the rice.
2. **Prepare the Roll:** Lay a nori sheet on a bamboo sushi mat, shiny side down. Spread a thin layer of sushi rice over the nori, leaving a small border at the top.
3. **Add the Fillings:** Place your chosen fillings horizontally in the middle of the rice.
4. **Roll the Sushi:** Roll the mat over the rice and fillings, pressing gently to form a tight roll.
5. **Slice and Serve:** Slice the roll into 6-8 pieces and serve with soy sauce.

Onigiri (Rice Balls)

Ingredients:

- 2 cups cooked short-grain rice
- 1 sheet nori, cut into strips
- Fillings of your choice (e.g., pickled plum, salmon, tuna mayo, etc.)
- Salt for seasoning

Instructions:

1. **Prepare the Rice:** While the rice is still warm, sprinkle a small amount of salt over the rice and mix it gently.
2. **Shape the Rice:** Wet your hands with water to prevent the rice from sticking. Take a handful of rice and mold it into a triangle or oval shape.
3. **Add the Filling:** Make a small indentation in the center of the rice and place your chosen filling inside. Close the rice around the filling to enclose it.
4. **Wrap the Onigiri:** Wrap a strip of nori around the base of the rice ball.
5. **Serve:** Enjoy as a snack or part of a meal.

Nikujaga (Beef and Potato Stew)

Ingredients:

- 1/2 lb thinly sliced beef (such as ribeye or sirloin)
- 3 medium potatoes, peeled and cut into wedges
- 1/2 onion, sliced
- 1/4 cup soy sauce
- 1/4 cup mirin
- 1/4 cup sugar
- 1 cup dashi broth
- 2 tablespoons vegetable oil

Instructions:

1. **Cook the Beef:** In a large pot, heat oil and sauté the beef until browned.
2. **Add the Vegetables:** Add the potatoes and onions to the pot and sauté for a few minutes.
3. **Add the Sauce:** Add the soy sauce, mirin, sugar, and dashi broth to the pot. Bring to a simmer, then cover and cook for 20-30 minutes, or until the potatoes are tender.
4. **Serve:** Serve hot over rice.

Tofu Katsu (Tofu Cutlet)

Ingredients:

- 1 block firm tofu, pressed and sliced into 1-inch thick slabs
- 1/2 cup flour
- 1 egg, beaten
- 1/2 cup panko breadcrumbs
- Vegetable oil for frying
- Tonkatsu sauce for serving

Instructions:

1. **Prepare the Tofu:** Press the tofu to remove excess water and slice it into 1-inch thick slabs.
2. **Breading the Tofu:** Coat each piece of tofu in flour, dip it in beaten egg, and then coat it in panko breadcrumbs.
3. **Fry the Tofu:** Heat vegetable oil in a pan over medium heat. Fry the tofu cutlets until golden and crispy on both sides.
4. **Serve:** Drain excess oil on paper towels and serve with tonkatsu sauce for dipping.

Unagi Don (Grilled Eel Rice Bowl)

Ingredients:

- 2 unagi (eel) fillets
- 2 cups cooked short-grain rice
- 2 tablespoons soy sauce
- 2 tablespoons mirin
- 1 tablespoon sugar
- 1 tablespoon sake
- 1 teaspoon sesame seeds (optional)
- Pickled ginger for garnish (optional)

Instructions:

1. **Prepare the Eel:** Preheat the grill or broiler. Brush the eel fillets with a mixture of soy sauce, mirin, sugar, and sake. Grill the eel for 5-7 minutes, basting occasionally with the sauce.
2. **Assemble the Bowl:** Place a portion of cooked rice in a bowl. Top with the grilled eel fillet.
3. **Garnish and Serve:** Drizzle more of the sauce over the eel and rice, and garnish with sesame seeds and pickled ginger if desired.

Chirashi Sushi (Scattered Sushi)

Ingredients:

- 2 cups sushi rice, cooked
- 1/4 cup rice vinegar
- 1 tablespoon sugar
- 1 teaspoon salt
- Assorted sashimi-grade fish (salmon, tuna, etc.), thinly sliced
- 1/4 cup cucumber, julienned
- 1/4 cup avocado, diced
- 1 sheet nori, shredded
- 1 tablespoon sesame seeds
- Pickled ginger and wasabi for serving

Instructions:

1. **Prepare the Rice:** Mix the rice vinegar, sugar, and salt in a small bowl until dissolved. Fold this mixture into the cooled sushi rice.
2. **Assemble the Chirashi:** Place the seasoned rice in a large bowl or individual bowls.
3. **Top with Fish and Garnishes:** Scatter the sliced sashimi-grade fish, cucumber, avocado, and shredded nori on top of the rice.
4. **Serve:** Sprinkle sesame seeds over the top and serve with pickled ginger and wasabi on the side.

Zaru Soba (Cold Soba Noodles)

Ingredients:

- 2 cups cooked soba noodles
- 1 tablespoon soy sauce
- 1 tablespoon mirin
- 1 teaspoon sugar
- 1/4 cup dashi broth
- 2 tablespoons chopped green onions
- Wasabi and nori strips for garnish

Instructions:

1. **Prepare the Noodles:** Cook the soba noodles according to package instructions. Drain and rinse under cold water to cool them.
2. **Prepare the Dipping Sauce:** In a small bowl, mix the soy sauce, mirin, sugar, and dashi broth.
3. **Serve:** Plate the soba noodles on a flat dish or bamboo mat. Serve the dipping sauce on the side, garnished with green onions, wasabi, and nori strips.

Nabe (Hot Pot)

Ingredients:

- 1/2 lb thinly sliced beef, chicken, or pork
- 1 cup napa cabbage, chopped
- 1 cup shiitake mushrooms, sliced
- 1/2 block tofu, cubed
- 2 cups dashi broth
- 2 tablespoons soy sauce
- 1 tablespoon mirin
- 1 tablespoon sake
- 1 tablespoon sesame oil

Instructions:

1. **Prepare the Broth:** In a large pot, combine dashi, soy sauce, mirin, and sake. Bring to a simmer.
2. **Add the Ingredients:** Add the meats, vegetables, tofu, and mushrooms to the pot. Let them cook for about 5-10 minutes or until tender.
3. **Serve:** Serve hot, with a side of dipping sauce or ponzu sauce, if desired.

Edamame (Steamed Soybeans)

Ingredients:

- 2 cups edamame (in pods)
- Sea salt for sprinkling

Instructions:

1. **Steam the Edamame:** Bring a pot of water to a boil and add the edamame. Boil for 4-5 minutes, or until tender.
2. **Serve:** Drain and sprinkle with sea salt. Serve warm as a snack or appetizer.

Ebi Tempura (Shrimp Tempura)

Ingredients:

- 12 large shrimp, peeled and deveined
- 1/2 cup all-purpose flour
- 1/2 cup cornstarch
- 1/2 teaspoon baking powder
- 1/2 cup ice-cold water
- Vegetable oil for frying
- Tempura dipping sauce for serving

Instructions:

1. **Prepare the Tempura Batter:** In a bowl, combine the flour, cornstarch, and baking powder. Add the ice-cold water and stir until just combined (lumps are okay).
2. **Heat the Oil:** Heat vegetable oil in a deep pan or fryer to 350°F (175°C).
3. **Coat and Fry the Shrimp:** Dip the shrimp into the batter and fry them in the hot oil until golden brown, about 2-3 minutes.
4. **Serve:** Drain the shrimp on paper towels and serve with tempura dipping sauce.

Kaiseki (Japanese Multi-Course Meal)

Ingredients:

- Various ingredients (seasonal fish, vegetables, rice, soup, etc.)
- Dashi stock
- Soy sauce
- Mirin
- Sake

Instructions:

1. **Course 1 (Appetizer):** Serve a small appetizer such as a light salad or small portion of seasonal vegetables.
2. **Course 2 (Soup):** Prepare a seasonal soup, typically miso or clear broth, served with tofu, mushrooms, and vegetables.
3. **Course 3 (Grilled Dish):** Grill a portion of fish or meat, such as grilled mackerel or teriyaki salmon.
4. **Course 4 (Sashimi):** Serve fresh sashimi with soy sauce and wasabi.
5. **Course 5 (Rice & Pickles):** Serve rice with pickles and a seasonal vegetable side dish.
6. **Course 6 (Dessert):** End with a light dessert, such as seasonal fruit or a small sweet.

Tori Karaage (Japanese Fried Chicken)

Ingredients:

- 1 lb chicken thighs, cut into bite-sized pieces
- 2 tablespoons soy sauce
- 1 tablespoon sake
- 1 tablespoon grated ginger
- 1 clove garlic, minced
- 1/4 cup potato starch or cornstarch
- Vegetable oil for frying

Instructions:

1. **Marinate the Chicken:** In a bowl, combine soy sauce, sake, grated ginger, and garlic. Add the chicken pieces and marinate for 30 minutes to 1 hour.
2. **Coat the Chicken:** Dredge the marinated chicken in potato starch or cornstarch.
3. **Fry the Chicken:** Heat vegetable oil in a pan over medium-high heat. Fry the chicken in batches until golden brown and crispy, about 3-4 minutes per batch.
4. **Serve:** Drain on paper towels and serve with lemon wedges.

Ebi Chili (Shrimp in Chili Sauce)

Ingredients:

- 1 lb shrimp, peeled and deveined
- 1 tablespoon vegetable oil
- 1/2 onion, chopped
- 2 cloves garlic, minced
- 2 tablespoons ketchup
- 1 tablespoon soy sauce
- 1 tablespoon chili paste or chili sauce
- 1 teaspoon sugar
- 1/2 cup water
- Green onions for garnish

Instructions:

1. **Cook the Shrimp:** Heat vegetable oil in a pan over medium heat. Add the shrimp and cook until pink and cooked through, about 2-3 minutes. Remove the shrimp from the pan and set aside.
2. **Prepare the Sauce:** In the same pan, sauté the onion and garlic until fragrant. Add ketchup, soy sauce, chili paste, and sugar, and cook for 2 minutes.
3. **Combine the Shrimp:** Return the shrimp to the pan and add water to create a saucy consistency. Stir to coat the shrimp.
4. **Serve:** Garnish with green onions and serve with rice.

Kushiage (Japanese Deep-Fried Skewers)

Ingredients:

- 1 lb pork, chicken, or vegetables (bell peppers, mushrooms, etc.), cut into bite-sized pieces
- 1/2 cup all-purpose flour
- 1 egg, beaten
- 1 cup panko breadcrumbs
- 1/4 cup soy sauce
- 1 tablespoon mirin
- 1 tablespoon sake
- 1 teaspoon sugar
- Vegetable oil for frying
- Skewers

Instructions:

1. **Prepare the Skewers:** Thread the meat or vegetables onto the skewers.
2. **Make the Coating:** Set up three bowls: one with flour, one with the beaten egg, and one with panko breadcrumbs.
3. **Coat the Skewers:** Dip each skewer in the flour, then the egg, and finally coat with panko breadcrumbs.
4. **Fry the Skewers:** Heat vegetable oil in a deep pan or fryer to 350°F (175°C). Fry the skewers in batches for 3-4 minutes until golden and crispy.
5. **Prepare the Dipping Sauce:** Mix soy sauce, mirin, sake, and sugar in a small bowl.
6. **Serve:** Serve the kushiage hot with the dipping sauce.

Goma-ae (Sesame Spinach Salad)

Ingredients:

- 1 lb spinach, blanched and drained
- 3 tablespoons sesame seeds
- 1 tablespoon sugar
- 2 teaspoons soy sauce
- 1 teaspoon mirin

Instructions:

1. **Prepare the Spinach:** Blanch the spinach in boiling water for 30 seconds, then drain and cool under cold water. Squeeze out excess moisture and chop into bite-sized pieces.
2. **Make the Sesame Sauce:** Toast the sesame seeds in a dry pan until fragrant. Grind them in a mortar and pestle or a spice grinder. Combine with sugar, soy sauce, and mirin to create a paste.
3. **Mix:** Toss the spinach with the sesame paste until well-coated.
4. **Serve:** Serve chilled as a side dish.

Hiyayakko (Chilled Tofu)

Ingredients:

- 1 block silken tofu
- 2 tablespoons soy sauce
- 1 teaspoon sesame oil
- 1 tablespoon green onions, chopped
- 1 tablespoon bonito flakes
- Fresh ginger, grated

Instructions:

1. **Prepare the Tofu:** Drain the tofu and cut it into cubes.
2. **Assemble:** Arrange the tofu in a shallow bowl.
3. **Top the Tofu:** Drizzle with soy sauce and sesame oil. Garnish with green onions, bonito flakes, and freshly grated ginger.
4. **Serve:** Serve cold as a refreshing appetizer or side dish.

Kinpira Gobo (Braised Burdock Root and Carrot)

Ingredients:

- 1 burdock root, peeled and julienned
- 1 carrot, peeled and julienned
- 1 tablespoon sesame oil
- 2 tablespoons soy sauce
- 1 tablespoon mirin
- 1 teaspoon sugar
- 1 tablespoon sesame seeds

Instructions:

1. **Prepare the Vegetables:** Peel and julienne the burdock root and carrot. Soak the burdock root in water with a little vinegar to prevent discoloration.
2. **Cook the Vegetables:** Heat sesame oil in a pan and stir-fry the burdock root and carrot for 5-7 minutes.
3. **Add the Sauce:** Add soy sauce, mirin, and sugar to the pan and cook for another 5 minutes until the liquid reduces.
4. **Serve:** Garnish with sesame seeds and serve as a side dish.

Japanese Curry

Ingredients:

- 1 lb chicken, beef, or pork, cut into chunks
- 2 onions, sliced
- 2 carrots, peeled and sliced
- 2 potatoes, peeled and cut into chunks
- 3 cups water or chicken broth
- 1 package Japanese curry roux (or curry powder)
- 2 tablespoons soy sauce
- 1 tablespoon mirin
- 1 tablespoon oil
- Cooked rice for serving

Instructions:

1. **Cook the Meat:** Heat oil in a pot and brown the chicken, beef, or pork. Remove and set aside.
2. **Sauté the Vegetables:** Add onions, carrots, and potatoes to the pot and sauté until softened.
3. **Add Broth and Curry Roux:** Add water or chicken broth and bring to a simmer. Stir in the curry roux or curry powder and soy sauce. Cook for about 30 minutes until the meat and vegetables are tender and the sauce thickens.
4. **Serve:** Serve the curry over cooked rice.

Takikomi Gohan (Seasoned Rice with Vegetables and Meat)

Ingredients:

- 2 cups short-grain rice
- 2 cups dashi broth
- 1/2 lb chicken thighs, cut into small pieces
- 1/2 cup shiitake mushrooms, sliced
- 1/4 cup carrots, julienned
- 1/4 cup soy sauce
- 2 tablespoons mirin
- 1 tablespoon sake

Instructions:

1. **Prepare the Rice:** Wash and drain the rice.
2. **Cook the Ingredients:** In a pot, combine the rice, dashi, chicken, mushrooms, and carrots. Add soy sauce, mirin, and sake.
3. **Simmer:** Bring to a boil, then reduce to a low simmer and cook for 15-20 minutes until the rice and chicken are fully cooked.
4. **Serve:** Fluff the rice and serve warm.

Oden (Japanese Hot Pot)

Ingredients:

- 2 cups dashi broth
- 2 boiled eggs
- 1/2 lb daikon radish, sliced
- 1/2 lb konnyaku (konjac), cut into pieces
- 1/2 lb fish cakes (chikuwa, odengyo)
- 1/2 lb tofu, cubed
- 2 tablespoons soy sauce
- 1 tablespoon mirin

Instructions:

1. **Prepare the Broth:** In a large pot, combine the dashi broth, soy sauce, and mirin. Bring to a simmer.
2. **Add the Ingredients:** Add the boiled eggs, daikon, konnyaku, fish cakes, and tofu to the pot. Simmer for 30-45 minutes, allowing the flavors to meld.
3. **Serve:** Serve hot with mustard on the side for dipping.

Chashu Pork (Braised Pork Belly)

Ingredients:

- 1 lb pork belly
- 2 tablespoons soy sauce
- 2 tablespoons mirin
- 1 tablespoon sake
- 1 tablespoon sugar
- 2 cloves garlic, crushed
- 1-inch piece ginger, sliced
- 2 cups water

Instructions:

1. **Sear the Pork:** Heat a pan and sear the pork belly on all sides until browned.
2. **Simmer:** In a pot, combine soy sauce, mirin, sake, sugar, garlic, ginger, and water. Add the pork belly and bring to a simmer. Cook for 1-1.5 hours until the pork is tender.
3. **Serve:** Slice the pork thinly and serve as a topping for ramen or rice.

Kakiage (Tempura Vegetable Fritters)

Ingredients:

- 1/2 cup shrimp, peeled and chopped
- 1/2 cup carrot, julienned
- 1/2 cup zucchini, julienned
- 1/2 onion, thinly sliced
- 1/2 cup tempura flour
- 1/4 cup cold water
- Vegetable oil for frying

Instructions:

1. **Prepare the Vegetables and Shrimp:** Mix the shrimp, carrot, zucchini, and onion in a bowl.
2. **Make the Batter:** In a separate bowl, combine tempura flour and cold water to make a light batter.
3. **Fry the Kakiage:** Heat oil in a deep pan. Drop spoonfuls of the batter mixture into the hot oil and fry for 2-3 minutes until golden and crispy.
4. **Serve:** Drain the kakiage on paper towels and serve with dipping sauce.

Mochi (Sweet Rice Cake)

Ingredients:

- 1 cup glutinous rice flour (mochi flour)
- 1/4 cup sugar
- 1/2 cup water
- Cornstarch (for dusting)

Instructions:

1. **Make the Dough:** In a heatproof bowl, mix the glutinous rice flour and sugar. Gradually add water, stirring to create a smooth batter.
2. **Steam the Mochi:** Cover the bowl with a damp cloth and steam the mixture for about 20-30 minutes, stirring halfway through. The dough will become sticky and translucent when done.
3. **Shape the Mochi:** Dust a clean surface with cornstarch. Once the dough has cooled slightly, transfer it to the surface and divide it into small pieces. Shape each piece into a ball or desired form.
4. **Serve:** Mochi can be eaten as is or filled with various fillings like red bean paste or ice cream.

Daifuku (Stuffed Mochi)

Ingredients:

- 1 cup glutinous rice flour (mochi flour)
- 1/4 cup sugar
- 1/2 cup water
- Cornstarch (for dusting)
- 1/2 cup sweet red bean paste (anko) or other fillings (like fruit or chocolate)

Instructions:

1. **Prepare the Mochi Dough:** In a bowl, combine glutinous rice flour and sugar, and gradually add water while stirring to create a smooth batter.
2. **Steam the Dough:** Cover and steam the mixture for 20-30 minutes, stirring halfway.
3. **Shape the Mochi:** Once cooled slightly, dust your work surface with cornstarch and divide the dough into small pieces. Flatten each piece into a round disc.
4. **Add Filling:** Place a small amount of sweet red bean paste (or your choice of filling) in the center of each disc and fold the edges over to seal.
5. **Serve:** Dust with more cornstarch if needed to prevent sticking. Enjoy fresh.

Anmitsu (Japanese Jelly Dessert)

Ingredients:

- 1 cup agar agar powder (or gelatin for an alternative)
- 3 cups water
- 1/4 cup sugar
- 1/2 cup sweet red bean paste (anko)
- 1/4 cup fruit (e.g., peach slices, cherries, or oranges)
- 2 tablespoons syrup (from fruit or simple syrup)
- Mochi or Shiratama dango (optional, for topping)

Instructions:

1. **Prepare Agar Agar:** In a saucepan, combine agar agar powder, sugar, and water. Bring to a boil while stirring, and simmer for a few minutes until the agar is fully dissolved.
2. **Set the Jelly:** Pour the mixture into a shallow dish or individual molds and let it cool in the refrigerator for about 1-2 hours to set.
3. **Assemble the Anmitsu:** Cut the set agar jelly into cubes.
4. **Serve:** Place the jelly cubes in a bowl, add sweet red bean paste, fruit, and optional toppings like mochi or Shiratama dango. Drizzle with syrup and serve chilled.

Taiyaki (Fish-Shaped Pancake)

Ingredients:

- 1 cup all-purpose flour
- 1 tablespoon sugar
- 1 teaspoon baking powder
- 1/4 teaspoon salt
- 1 egg
- 1/2 cup milk
- 1/4 cup water
- 1 tablespoon vegetable oil
- 1/2 cup sweet red bean paste (anko) or custard filling (optional)

Instructions:

1. **Make the Batter:** In a bowl, mix flour, sugar, baking powder, and salt. In another bowl, whisk together the egg, milk, water, and oil. Combine the wet and dry ingredients, and stir to form a smooth batter.
2. **Prepare the Taiyaki Mold:** Preheat a taiyaki mold (fish-shaped waffle maker) and lightly grease it.
3. **Cook the Taiyaki:** Pour a small amount of batter into the mold to cover the bottom, add a spoonful of red bean paste (or custard) in the center, then cover with more batter. Close the mold and cook for 3-4 minutes per side, until golden brown.
4. **Serve:** Serve warm, and enjoy the crispy, golden exterior with the sweet filling inside.

Matcha Cake

Ingredients:

- 1 1/2 cups all-purpose flour
- 2 tablespoons matcha powder
- 1 teaspoon baking powder
- 1/2 cup butter, softened
- 1 cup sugar
- 2 large eggs
- 1/2 cup milk
- 1 teaspoon vanilla extract
- A pinch of salt

Instructions:

1. **Preheat the Oven:** Preheat your oven to 350°F (175°C). Grease and flour a cake pan.
2. **Mix Dry Ingredients:** In a bowl, sift the flour, matcha powder, baking powder, and salt.
3. **Cream the Butter and Sugar:** In another bowl, beat the butter and sugar together until light and fluffy.
4. **Add the Eggs and Milk:** Add the eggs one at a time, beating well after each addition. Stir in the milk and vanilla extract.
5. **Combine Wet and Dry Ingredients:** Gradually fold the dry ingredients into the wet ingredients, mixing until smooth.
6. **Bake:** Pour the batter into the prepared cake pan and bake for 25-30 minutes, or until a toothpick comes out clean.
7. **Serve:** Allow to cool before serving. You can top with whipped cream or powdered sugar for extra flavor.

Yuzu Sorbet

Ingredients:

- 1 cup yuzu juice (or yuzu concentrate)
- 1 cup water
- 1/2 cup sugar
- 1 tablespoon lemon juice (optional, for extra tartness)

Instructions:

1. **Prepare the Simple Syrup:** In a saucepan, heat water and sugar over medium heat, stirring until the sugar dissolves. Remove from heat and let cool.
2. **Mix the Ingredients:** Once the syrup is cool, add the yuzu juice and lemon juice (if using).
3. **Freeze the Sorbet:** Pour the mixture into a shallow dish and place it in the freezer. Every 30 minutes, stir the sorbet with a fork to break up any ice crystals. Continue stirring until the mixture is frozen and smooth, about 3-4 hours.
4. **Serve:** Serve the yuzu sorbet in chilled bowls for a refreshing treat.

www.ingramcontent.com/pod-product-compliance
Lightning Source LLC
LaVergne TN
LVHW081505060526
838201LV00056BA/2940